The TECHNOLOGY BOOK for GIRLS

and Other Advanced Beings

written by
Trudee Romanek

illustrated by
Pat Cupples

KIDS CAN PRESS

To my children, Graham, Brina and Scott, whose curiosity inspires me to learn new things every day — T.R.

Acknowledgments

My utmost thanks to the many people who volunteered their time and expertise to assist me in gathering information, particularly the women profiled within the book and those whose names follow: Ian Lang of Barrie North Collegiate, Barrie, Ontario; the staff of the Barrie Public Library; Dr. Greg McWatt and the staff of the Baywood Animal Hospital, Barrie; Mike Hoare and Tony Tam of Bell Mobility; Courtney Kanerva of BRK Brands Canada; Dennis Mark of Calhoon's Restaurant, Barrie; Vickie Davis of Carlton Cards; M. Elizabeth Dann and Melody Reynolds of Corning Incorporated; Doug Little of FLIR Systems Incorporated; David Goff of Force, Incorporated; the staff of the Future Shop, Barrie; Hugh Bissett of the Integrated Manufacturing Technologies Institute (National Research Council of Canada); Kathi Haas of Motorola; Jean-Guy Monette and the staff of the National Museum of Science and Technology, Canada; Steve Watson of NCR Canada Ltd.; Professor Carolyn Merry of the Ohio State University; Xijia Gu of the Ontario Laser and Lightwave Research Centre; Jason Northedge of RCA; Constable Bill Braun of the RCMP; Sid Lee of the Royal Astronomical Society of Canada, Calgary Centre; Lynn Haywood McLean of the Royal Bank of Canada; Dr. Rob Ballagh and Paul Swain of the Royal Victoria Hospital, Barrie; Kevin Aver of Sensormatic; Ed Jones of Sloan Valve Company; Gail G. Mattson and the Society of Women Engineers; Michael Gulin of Sony Canada; Professor Lambertus Hesselink of Stanford University; Alan Goldenberg of Sterling-Semed Electronics; Francie Mendelsohn of Summit Research Associates; Robert Gumiela of Toshiba of Canada Ltd.; Professor Ken Pohlmann of the University of Miami; Ken Cole of World Dryer Canada; Carol J. Amato; Dr. Vaughn Becker; Dr. Roberta L. Bondar; Elizabeth Cannon; Karen Krossing; Mary Ellen Ridley; Sandra Shimizu and David Herr; and David Thorman.

Special thanks to my editor, Liz, for her ability to read my thoughts … and correct them, to Julia, whose design helps make these abstract concepts so much clearer, to Pat for her charming illustrations, and to my husband, Rob, for his enthusiasm and terrific suggestions, and for believing in me.

Thanks to the following organizations or individuals for permission to use the photos that appear in this book: p. 11, FLIR Systems Incorporated; p. 21, Ken Pohlmann of the University of Miami Music Engineering; p. 27, NASA; p. 41, Corning Incorporated.

Kids Can Press acknowledges the financial support of the Ontario Arts Council, the Canada Council for the Arts and the Government of Canada, through the BPIDP, for our publishing activity.

Published in Canada by
Kids Can Press Ltd.
29 Birch Avenue
Toronto, ON M4V 1E2

Published in the U.S. by
Kids Can Press Ltd.
2250 Military Road
Tonawanda, NY 14150

Edited by Elizabeth MacLeod
Designed by Julia Naimska
Printed and bound in Hong Kong by Book Art Inc., Toronto

CM 01 0 9 8 7 6 5 4 3 2 1
CM PA 01 0 9 8 7 6 5 4 3 2 1

Canadian Cataloguing in Publication Data

Romanek, Trudee
    The technology book for girls : and other advanced beings

Includes index.
ISBN 1-55074-936-6 (bound) ISBN 1-55074-619-7 (pbk.)

1. Technology — Juvenile literature. 2. Technology — Experiments — Juvenile literature. 3. Women in technology — Juvenile literature. I. Cupples, Patricia. II. Title.

T48.R65 2001   j604'.8'342   C00-931792-9

Kids Can Press is a Nelvana company

CONTENTS

WHAT IS TECHNOLOGY?

"What topic did you get?" asks Gina. Her friend Kirsten is anxiously unfolding a slip of paper she has drawn from a bowl.

"How Dolphins Communicate," Kirsten reads from the slip of paper.

Gina whispers, "Hey, that's not too bad, for a science project."

"Gina?" calls Ms. Koffler, the science teacher. "Your turn."

Gina takes a deep breath and reaches into the bowl. She unfolds her slip of paper and silently reads the words written there. In disbelief, she reads them again.

"Your topic, Gina?" Ms. Koffler asks.

"Advanced Technology in Our Everyday Lives," Gina replies, sounding more than a little worried.

The bell rings and Gina's classmates start packing up their books.

"All right, class," Ms. Koffler announces, "your projects are due in four weeks."

Gina turns to Kirsten. "Advanced technology? What does that mean? I don't even know what regular technology is!" she groans.

Ms. Koffler comes over. "Concerned about your project, Gina?"

"Kind of. What exactly do you mean by advanced technology. Like, space shuttles?"

"That is advanced technology, but people don't use it every day," replies the teacher. "Technology is using the science you know to get something done. You know that magnets attract metal objects, right? Well, if you use a magnet to remove paper clips from a bucket of sand, that would be technology. Any tool is an example of technology."

"So, you want me to do my project on tools?"

"Not just any tools. 'Advanced technology' usually means the complex tools and machines that have been invented more recently,"

explains Ms. Koffler. "They probably use electricity and many of them may seem almost like magic if you don't know how they work.

"Most people don't realize that they use many very advanced tools all the time," Ms. Koffler continues. "I'd like you to find out about some of those for your project."

"But ... how will I find these things?" questions Gina, panic creeping into her voice.

"Look around you carefully, at home and in places you visit. Ask yourself how each thing you see works. If you're not sure, check with someone who might know." She pauses, seeing the worried expression on Gina's face. "Come and talk to me if you're having trouble," she adds, "but I know you can handle this topic."

As the two girls reach the hallway, Gina heaves a sigh and turns to Kirsten.

"I think it's going to be a long four weeks."

SILENT SIGNALS

Gina plunks herself down on the living room sofa. Where can she possibly find advanced technology in her house? Deep in thought, she hardly notices her little sister, Sophie, leaping around the room. Soon, however, the din of constantly changing channels on the television interrupts her concentration.

"Sophie, what are you doing?" Gina demands.

"Beware of my intergalactic space zapper!" growls Sophie, pointing the TV remote at Gina.

"Cut it out, would ya? The TV's going crazy …" Gina stops, staring at the remote. "I wonder how this tells our TV what to do?" Then a thought strikes her: Maybe it uses advanced technology!

"Mom?" Gina calls, grabbing her backpack. "Is it okay if I go to the electronics store down the street? I'll be back before supper."

The front of a remote control device sends out an infrared beam that carries a message. Even though your eyes can't see infrared, a small opening on the front of the TV or VCR can.

The television "sees" the beam, and inside the TV a microchip — the part that acts like the TV's "brain" — receives the message and makes the TV respond.

WHAT IS INFRARED?

Every object — a person, a wooden table, a metal car — is made of microscopic bits called molecules and atoms. These bits are always moving.

As the bits move and bump into each other, they give off heat. Heat is really a type of energy called infrared radiation. The faster the bits move, the more infrared radiation the object gives off. Even frozen objects contain these moving bits, but they're moving much more slowly.

Scientists invented a way to send a stream of infrared out a small hole at the front of your TV remote. Each button on the remote produces a different pattern of infrared pulses, so the remote can signal the TV to change channels rather than turn off, for instance.

FEEL THE HEAT

If infrared is heat, you should be able to feel it, right? Put your hand in front of your TV remote, then press a button. Feel any heat? Probably not. It takes very little infrared radiation to tell your TV what it needs to know. Trying to feel that bit of heat is like trying to hear someone whisper a block away. Your senses just aren't sensitive enough.

To really sense infrared, take a look at your toaster.

1. Turn the toaster on.

2. Place your hand about 30 cm (1 ft.) above the toaster, and watch what happens inside.

Soon after you turn the toaster on, even before its elements begin to glow, you should be able to feel the heat. That's because the elements are giving off much more infrared radiation than a remote control.

(KEEP ALL PARTS OF YOU, INCLUDING YOUR HAIR, A SAFE DISTANCE FROM THE TOASTER SO YOU WON'T GET BURNED.)

CONTROL YOUR REMOTE

Test your remote control to see how infrared behaves.

You'll need:

▶ a friend
▶ a television with a remote control device
▶ white paper
▶ black construction paper (it must be very black and not shiny)

1. Turn the TV on. Take two large steps away from it.

2. Have your friend stand one step farther from the TV and a little to one side of you, holding the white piece of paper in front of her.

3. Point the remote control device at the paper, about 5 cm (2 in.) away. Now press the button to change the channel. What happens?

4. Ask your friend to hold the black paper in the same spot. What happens when you press the button?

The white paper bounces the infrared beam so the TV gets the message. The black paper absorbs the infrared, stopping the message. (If your black paper bounces the beam, it may not be black enough. Try a Teflon pan.)

RADIATION RELATIVES

Infrared radiation is part of the electromagnetic spectrum. This spectrum includes many kinds of energy that travel in waves. White light and colored light — the only types of wave energy that humans can see — make up just a tiny slice of that spectrum. (White light is all colors of light combined.)

The waves of energy that make the color purple, or violet, are the shortest that humans can see. The waves that make red are the longest humans see. The other colors fall in between. Beyond red is infrared, with waves even longer than red's. (Beyond violet is ultraviolet, which is also invisible to people.)

Infrared behaves the way light behaves. It bounces off light things better than off dark things. Bouncing light is what makes a white snowbank so dazzlingly bright to look at.

NOW YOU SEE IT, NOW YOU DON'T

With an adult's permission, point a video camera at a remote control as a friend presses and holds its buttons. Turn on the camera, look through it and you'll see a light coming from the remote. Even though the human eye can't see infrared, the special equipment in the camera senses it and makes it visible.

Remotely Interested

Diana Laboy-Rush is an electrical engineer. The company she works for in California, USA, makes computer chips that are put inside many products — television remotes, computer modems, even toys.

Diana is an infrared specialist — she develops new products that use infrared to do a new task. Diana has designed many products, including a remote that lets people send e-mail from a TV screen.

ALARMING DISCOVERIES

On Saturday morning, Gina wanders sleepily to the kitchen. Her parents look up from the newspaper and say good morning. Behind them, a thin stream of smoke begins to rise from the toaster on the counter.

Suddenly, the smoke detector on the ceiling lets out an ear-piercing squeal. Roscoe barks in surprise and Gina's mom runs to free the burning toast. Gina's dad frantically waves a dishtowel at the smoke detector as Gina struggles to open a window. After a few moments the air clears and the squealing stops. Gina looks up at the smoke detector.

"Dad? How did the smoke detector know the toast was burning?"

"Well, the smoke goes up and, uh, ... Let's stop at the firehall and see if your Aunt Jo can help answer this one."

Most homes and buildings contain photoelectronic smoke alarms that use infrared beams. Inside most alarms, an infrared beam shines away from a special receptor. As long as the beam doesn't reach the receptor, the alarm is quiet.

When tiny smoke particles enter the alarm, they float into the beam and reflect some of the infrared signal toward the receptor. As more particles enter, the receptor receives more infrared beam. That triggers the alarm to go off.

In another type of alarm, the infrared beam shines toward the

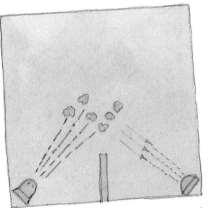

receptor. When enough smoke particles enter the detector, they reflect the beam away from the receptor and that sets off the alarm.

THE FLIR

The Forward-Looking InfraRed, or FLIR, is a camera with a sensitive infrared sensor. It picks up the natural infrared radiation given off by people and other warm objects and makes it visible on a special screen. It works especially well after dark, when the heat of the Sun doesn't hide the heat of people.

Search and rescue workers use the FLIR to find people lost in the wilderness. Police use it to track down runaway criminals. The FLIR also helps firefighters find any hot spots left after a forest fire.

BEAM BREAKERS

A burglar creeps toward the jewels in the display case and puts on special goggles. Suddenly, she can see dozens of beams crisscrossing around the jewels. If any beam is broken, an alarm goes off.

Some automatic garage doors have a safety feature that works almost the same way. An invisible infrared beam shines from one side of the doorway to a receptor in the other side. As long as the beam reaches the receptor, the door can close.

If a person (or an object) is in the path of the door, the invisible beam is broken. This stops the door from closing so it won't hurt anyone or damage anything.

OPEN SESAME

"So, smoke alarms and TV remotes both use infrared," says Gina, heading for the mall with her dad and Sophie. "This project might not be so bad after all!"

Sophie runs up to the entrance, then waits for the doors to open. Gina stares at the small black box above the doors.

"Somehow that box knew Sophie wanted to go in," she says. "I wonder how."

"Maybe there's a beam, like in a smoke detector," Sophie suggests.

"But the detector had one part to send the beam and another part to receive it," replies Gina. "Where's the receiving part for the doors?"

"Let's ask him," Gina's dad says, pointing to the repairman behind her.

The infrared beam shines out of that box above the doors. Another part of the box holds the receptor. Some doors have the infrared parts in the frame. You can't see a box, just some holes.

When you get close to the doors, your body reflects the beam back to the box. The beam hits the receptor and triggers the doors to open.

INVISIBLE DOORMAN

Find a building that has an automatic door without any floormats in metal frames. (That type works differently.) When it's not busy, ask the manager if you can test it.

1. Approach the door and stop walking as soon as it opens. (Stay far enough back that it won't hit you if it closes.) Did it stay open?

2. This time, stop once you are just through the doorway. Watch the door. Be ready to move out of the way if it begins to close.

Some doors have one sensor. It opens the door as you approach and may hold it open as long as you stand in front of the door. Once you step inside, the sensor lets the door close. Or a timer may keep the door open a few seconds, then let it close even if you're still there.

Other doors have two or three sensors to "see" you as you go in. They hold the door open so it won't close on someone still in the doorway.

If the door you tested stayed open while you stood just inside, it probably had more than one sensor. Look above the door and see if you can find the sensor units that were "watching" you.

Space Predictions

Space is filled with glowing stars, but there are many other objects in space that aren't hot enough to glow. And if they don't glow, you can't see them, even with a regular telescope. So astronomer Helen Walker uses an infrared telescope.

Helen studies space dust at the Rutherford Appleton Laboratory near Oxford, England. Her infrared telescope picks up the tiny amounts of infrared given off by the dust and, with a computer, lets Helen see it. By studying the dust, she helps other scientists discover how planets form and predict the future of stars like our Sun.

BATHROOM BEAMS

"Gina!" her mom calls. "There's some e-mail for you. Something about hand dryers?"

Gina races in. "Finally, maybe I'll find out how these things work. Kirsten and I searched on the Internet all Saturday afternoon and couldn't find a thing."

"Hand dryers?" Her mom looks surprised. "You push the button and they start. What's there to understand about them?"

Gina shakes her head. "Not the ones at the mall. You just stick your hands under them and they go on. I think they might use infrared, like the automatic doors. I wrote down the name of the company that makes them and sent an e-mail to ask them how the dryers work."

16:08 PM
Message
From: pat@bathsmartz.com
Subject: Hand dryers
Attachment:

Dear Gina: I'm an engineer at BathSmartz. Our automatic hand dryers use an infrared beam to find out if there are hands under them waiting to be dried. A cone of invisible infrared "shines" from a dark circle under the dryer all the time. The beam focuses at the point where most people place their hands. If you put your hands there, they reflect the beam back.

Another part of the dryer, called the photo transistor, receives the reflected light and tells the dryer to turn on. When you move your hands away, the beam is not reflected anymore, and, after a moment, the dryer turns off. Hope that helps!

P.S. We make water taps that work the same way.

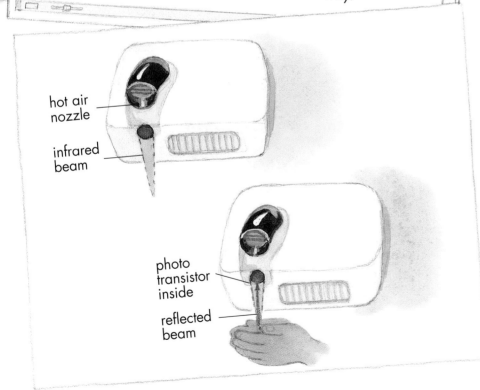

hot air nozzle

infrared beam

photo transistor inside

reflected beam

PHANTOM FLUSHER

Ever seen a toilet flush by itself? Here's how it works. Part of the toilet's equipment is mounted in the wall behind the bowl. It constantly sends out an infrared beam to the area above the bowl.

When you sit down, the beam is reflected back to a sensor in the wall unit and the toilet "knows" you're there. When you get up, the beam isn't reflected anymore. The toilet waits a few seconds and then, whoosh, flushes by itself.

TOYS THAT TALK BACK

In 1997, Mattel created the Talk with Me Barbie doll. Hook the doll's "computer" up to a real one and, after some time at her workstation, this Barbie doll is ready to carry on a conversation. At least that's how it seems.

Once you tell your real computer what you want your Barbie doll to say, her "computer" sends infrared signals to pass the message on to her. An infrared sensor in her necklace receives the information and a computer chip inside the doll sorts it out.

LASERS IN THE LIBRARY

"Doing a project, Gina?" the school librarian asks.

"Trying to, Mr. Ford," she replies. *"I've learned lots about infrared, but I need some other advanced technologies we use."*

Mr. Ford begins to check out Gina's books.

"Would a laser count? That's what this is," he explains as he shines a skinny red line of light onto the bar code of the first book.

"A laser? Really? How does it work?" asks Gina.

"I'll bet we have a book that explains it," Mr. Ford says, heading for the shelves. *"You know, lasers do many things,"* he continues. *"They even record music."*

WHAT'S A LASER?

A laser is a device that produces a very concentrated beam of light. Inside the laser is a chamber containing a crystal or gas. When energy is pumped into the chamber, the bits of the crystal absorb the energy and give off small bursts of light.

The bursts of light, called photons, fall in line with one another and move together across the chamber. At one end, they bounce off a very reflective mirror. At the other end is a partial mirror that can reflect light but can also let a beam of light through if it's strong enough. As more energy is pumped into the chamber, more photons fall in line until a strong laser beam shines out through the partial mirror.

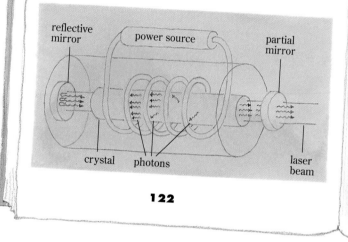

reflective mirror · power source · partial mirror · crystal · photons · laser beam

This beam of light is different from other sources of light. The waves of light from the Sun or a lightbulb scatter in many directions, but waves of laser light all move together in the same direction. Also, the gas or crystal produces light in only one wavelength, so the waves are all the same color. (Light from the Sun or a lightbulb is made up of all colors of light.)

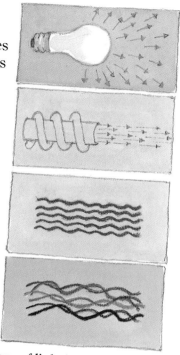

A beam of laser light doesn't spread out like the light from a lightbulb. That makes it good for sending light signals and scanning bar codes. Laser light can also be concentrated, making some laser beams strong enough to cut through almost anything.

WHAT'S IN A NAME?

The laser gets its name from the phrase Light Amplification by Stimulated Emission of Radiation. The beam of laser light is amplified (increased) when the gas or crystal in the chamber is stimulated by the energy being pumped in. It emits (gives off) more and more photons, which are a form of radiation.

Bar Code Scanners

In a library that has a laser scanner, each book is given a number. That number, as well as the book's title, author and publisher, are entered into the library's computer.

Each person who uses the library has a number on a library card and the computer is given information to go with each user number — the person's name and address.

The bar code on a book or a library card is just another way to show its number. When you check out a book, the librarian scans the bar code on your card to let the computer know who you are and then scans the bar code on the book.

The scanner sends out a thin strip of laser light. Inside the scanner, a receptor senses the light that reflects back. When the laser light hits a bar code, it is absorbed by the black lines but bounces off the white spaces in between. The wider the white space is, the more light gets reflected back to the receptor. The wider the black bar, the longer the space where no light is reflected.

The scanner translates the light and spaces into the bar code number and lets the computer know which item is being scanned. The computer then has a record of the items you've checked out.

Some stores use laser scanners, too. The bar code on each store item tells the cash register how much to charge for it and lets the store computer keep track of which items have been sold and how many are left.

Lasers are used in scanners because laser light doesn't spread out the way light from a lightbulb does. It stays in a very straight, even line. That means the light is reflected back in a very straight, even line that is easy for the receptor to read.

SPEED SCANNING

Grocery scanners are a lot like library scanners, except the laser light shines out of a scanner in the counter. The cashier passes each item, bar code down, over the scanner before he bags it. If the cashier had to stop and shine a light on each item, as in the library, his job would go a lot slower.

In future, each bar code may be printed on a label with a tiny antenna in it. As a customer pushes a cart past the checkout, a cashier will be able to scan all the items in the cart at once.

POLLY WANTS A BAR CODE

Ever chatted with a talking parrot? At first it may seem smart, but soon you realize that it can only say what it's been taught to say. Store cash registers and library computers are the same: they only "know" what's been programmed into them.

Want to prove it? Call the manager of a store that has a laser scanner to ask if you can run a short test on it. Take with you two bar-coded items that the store doesn't sell. Ask the cashier if you may watch the computer screen as she scans other people's items. What information appears? Now ask her to scan your items. What does the computer tell you?

Laser Pioneer

When Elsa Garmire was a physics student in the early 1960s, there was only one laser in the world. Then her supervisor bought the world's second laser. Elsa was one of the first people to experiment with laser light. Without her research, CD players and laser printers couldn't have been developed.

Elsa is now a professor at the Thayer School of Engineering in New Hampshire, USA. Today she uses lasers to help computers "recognize" and respond to images as quickly as people's brains do. Soon, the computers may be able to examine patients' X rays or find defective parts in a factory.

TURNING MUSIC INTO LIGHT

"Whatcha doin', Gina?" asks Sophie, bouncing into the room.

"Looking at this CD. Mr. Ford said lasers have something to do with recording music." She glances at Sophie. "You wouldn't understand. Why don't you go play?"

"Okay, fine," Sophie huffs. She heads out of the room, talking as she goes. "Mom says lasers turn music into light to make a CD. She's got pictures of it in a music magazine. But if you don't want to know ..."

Gina's head snaps up. "What magazine? Sophie? Sophie!"

THE DISC

To make a music CD, or compact disc, a recording company starts with a glass disc about the same size as a CD. Spread across the top of the disc is a chemical that's sensitive to light.

A computer-controlled laser produces a beam of energy that's focused to a point many times smaller than a pinprick. The laser shines onto the glass disc, starting near the hole in its center. As the disc turns around and around, the laser turns on and off, exposing tiny areas of the disc (like light exposing camera film) in a long spiraling line called a track.

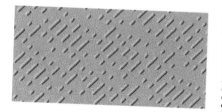

This is a microscope picture of some pits on a compact disc. The section of about 20 tracks is not as wide as one hair.

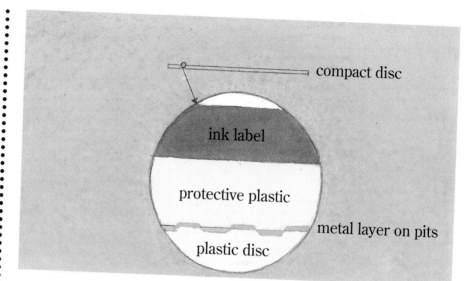

compact disc

ink label

protective plastic

metal layer on pits

plastic disc

Later, when the chemical is developed, these exposed areas turn into dents in the disc called pits. The flat areas that were not exposed are called lands. This glass master disc is then used to make thousands of plastic copies. The top side of each one is coated with a thin layer of shiny metal. A layer of plastic goes on next to protect it. Then the label is printed on top and the discs are ready to sell in music stores.

THE MUSIC

Ever heard of Morse code? In this code, each letter of the alphabet is represented by a combination of dots and dashes. Computer data is a little like that. Every letter, every sound, every speck of a picture can be translated into a combination of 0s and 1s. To record a music CD, a computer changes the music into this code. Then the computer sends this long

continued on next page

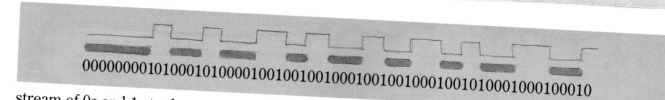

0000000010100010100001001001001000100100100010010100010001000100010

stream of 0s and 1s to the recording machine.

The 0s and 1s of the music tell the laser when to turn on and off. When the machine receives the first 1 in the code, the laser comes on to begin a pit. For every 0 that follows, the pit is made longer until the next 1 comes along. That 1 tells the laser to turn off, which ends the pit and starts a land. The land stretches until another 1 comes along, which begins a new pit. The machine continues, changing from pit to land or land to pit whenever it receives a 1 from the computer.

PLAYBACK TIME

Lasers change music into 0s and 1s to record it, but did you know lasers also change those 0s and 1s back into music?

Inside every compact disc player is a laser. While the CD player spins the disc, the laser shines up onto the disc's bottom surface. The laser light passes through the clear plastic and hits the shiny metal coating above the pits and lands.

More light reflects back through the flat lands than through the pits. A light sensor, called a photodiode, receives those reflections and passes the information along to the computer processor in the CD player. The processor changes the information back into the code of 0s and 1s and from that code into the music that created the patterns in the first place.

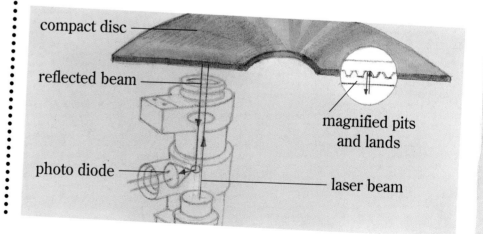

compact disc

reflected beam

photo diode

magnified pits and lands

laser beam

THEN AND NOW

Before there were lasers and compact discs, people used other methods to record music onto vinyl record albums and cassette tapes. Why are most recording companies now using compact discs?

CDs are stronger and last longer than records or tapes. Also, they can hold more music, since the tiny pits of laser-recorded information take up so little space. A compact disc can hold more than an hour of music. A vinyl record, nearly three times as large and recorded on both sides, holds less.

Lasers record more than just music onto CDs. Computer software, photographs, even books are being recorded onto compact discs. One CD can hold 300 long novels, 5000 pictures or 5 minutes of your favorite television program. It can also hold as much information as 1500 traditional computer floppy discs contain.

Soon everyone may be listening to music recorded onto CDs using MP3 computer software. MP3 songs are so compressed that more than 100 of them will fit on a compact disc.

HOW SMALL IS SMALL?

Pits on a disc are extremely shallow. A fingerprint — just that thin layer of oil that your finger leaves behind — sticks up 30 times higher than the depth of a pit.

ALL WOUND UP

If you could stretch out the recorded track of a CD, it would be about 5.5 km (3$\frac{1}{2}$ miles) long!

HOW IS A CD LIKE A MOVIE?

Did you know that movies are made of thousands of pictures that flash quickly onto the screen one after the other? Your brain runs the pictures all together and the action on the screen seems to be moving continuously.

Music on a compact disc is a little like a movie. It's recorded digitally, which means the recorder records many tiny snippets of the music. When the thousands of snippets per second are played back, your brain can't tell them apart. It strings them together, like movie pictures, and you hear them as continuous sound.

TECHNOLOGY IN YOUR POCKET

"Guess what, Dad? There's a laser in our CD player!"

"Really? I didn't know that," says Gina's dad. He thinks for a minute. "You know, there's a laser in the printer hooked up to your mom's computer, too. And see this credit card?" he continues, pulling out his wallet. "That shiny picture that changes when I tilt it is a hologram. Lasers make those. Come to think of it, I have a laser in my pocket. I bought it today for my work presentations."

"In your pocket?" Gina asks, amazed. "Cool! Let's see it."

Congratulations! You now own a Make Your Point Laser Key Chain. Just aim this handy accessory at your wall chart or projector screen and press the button. Instantly, a thin laser beam travels invisibly across the room, highlighting whatever you wish in a red spot of light. Used by executives around the world. CAUTION! DO NOT STARE INTO BEAM. LASER RADIATION CAN DAMAGE EYES. ————

MAKING THE INVISIBLE VISIBLE

Shine a flashlight into a cloudless night sky. See how the light seems to just disappear? Try a daytime experiment with a laser pointer or a flashlight to find out why.
NEVER SHINE A LASER INTO ANYONE'S EYES.

You'll need:

▶ a friend
▶ a laser pointer or flashlight
▶ a shaker of talcum powder

1. Stand with your laser pointer or flashlight a step or two to one side of an open doorway. Slightly open the shaker of talcum powder and hold it in your other hand.

2. Position a friend outside the doorway. Shine your light across the doorway onto the opposite wall. Can you see your light? Ask your friend if she can see it.

3. With the light still on, sprinkle powder in the doorway so it falls into the beam of light. Can your friend see the light now?

PICTURES OF LIGHT

Holograms, such as the ones on many credit cards, are three-dimensional pictures. To make a hologram, a laser beam is split into a pair of identical beams.

One beam shines on a piece of photographic film in front of the object. The other beam reflects off the object onto the film. The beams come together again at the film and how they bump into each other is recorded there. The pattern they make creates the hologram when the film is developed. Only laser light can be split into a pair of beams and brought back together to record a hologram.

Holograms cannot be copied using a photocopy machine. So most credit cards and even money in some countries, such as Canada and Australia, have holograms to make them difficult to counterfeit.

A beam of light is invisible in air. You can only see it when it reflects (bounces) off something. Laser light is the same. You could see your light hit the wall in front of you and reflect off it. Your friend could see the light only when the particles of powder in the air reflected it.

HARDWORKING LASERS

"So, Ms. Koffler sent you to me," says Mr. Heath, the factory foreman. "She's right about lasers. They can be powerful. A laser beam of the right wavelength can cut almost anything. Some can even cut diamonds."

"What do you use them for here?" Gina yells over the noise.

"We make cars, so we use lasers to cut metal parts and also to weld them together.

Now, if you go across the road, they've got different lasers there that drill tiny holes in baby bottle nipples."

"Why not just use a drill?" asks Gina.

"Laser cuts leave smooth edges. Nothing has to be sanded. Plus, drill bits and saws wear down or get dull from rubbing as they cut. A laser is just powerful light!"

LOOKING FOR LASER EDGES

You may have some laser-cut cloth in your closet. Look at the labels in a few of your sweaters and shirts. Examine the edges of each tag, with a magnifying glass if you have one. What do you see? Any edges that are frayed or folded and stitched were probably cut traditionally.

What about the other labels? Can you find any that are stiff and shiny, perhaps a bit rounded or scratchy? If you can, you are probably looking at an edge that has been cut and melted by a laser.

THE POWER OF LASERS

"So, there's no blade to wear out?" asks Gina's mom.

"Right," Mr. Heath replies. "Lasers are faster, too, because they're usually more powerful and accurate. I once worked in a clothing factory with a laser that cut through 500 layers of cloth at once. If the cloth was synthetic, such as polyester or nylon, the laser would even melt the edge so it wouldn't unravel."

LUNAR LASER

Laser light travels at the speed of light. Scientists used that fact and a laser to measure how far it is from Earth to the Moon. They shone a laser at the Moon and timed how long it took the beam to reflect back. Then they used that time and the speed to calculate the distance.

And how does the Moon reflect the laser light? In 1969, Apollo 11 astronauts placed a mirror on the Moon to do the job.

A laser beam doesn't cut the way a knife does. Instead, it pours huge amounts of energy into the material, burning away whatever lies directly in its path. The beam of the first laser ever made had 10 000 times as much energy as a beam of sunlight.

Different lasers produce different wavelengths of energy. To do its job, a laser has to produce the right kind of energy. Blue laser light won't have much effect on an object that doesn't absorb blue light. The energy would just bounce off or pass right through.

LASERS IN MEDICINE

"Gina! Wait up. I've got something for your project!" Kirsten calls. "My dad wants to have surgery to get rid of his glasses. But my mom doesn't want him to do it. She says new glasses are a lot cheaper."

"Your dad's glasses are advanced technology?" asks Gina.

"No, no," Kirsten explains, "Dad says Dr. Wong's going to use lasers to fix his eyes. I brought brochures from her office."

"Thanks! Speaking of lasers, do you know where I put my dad's laser pointer after that powder experiment? I can't find it anywhere."

IMPROVE YOUR EYESIGHT

Cornea removed to correct nearsightedness

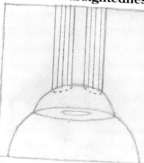

Cornea removed to correct farsightedness

Many eye surgeons now offer a procedure that can improve some people's vision so much they no longer need eyeglasses or contact lenses. The surgery is performed with a computerized laser.

The beam from this specially adapted laser can remove microscopic amounts of tissue in just the right places. This reshapes the cornea, the front of the eye, so that it bends the rays of light the correct amount, allowing the person to see.

CATCHING A WAVE

Scientists have figured out which body tissues absorb which wavelengths of energy. Think about a red shirt. It looks red because it absorbs most of the blue, green and yellow wavelengths but reflects back the red. Different laser light is reflected or absorbed by different body tissues, too. Doctors use a laser whose energy will be absorbed by the tissue they are operating on.

For eye surgery, doctors use a laser whose energy is absorbed by the tissue at the front of the eye. These lasers "cut" by focusing their energy on just a few cells at a time. The intense energy turns the liquid inside each cell to steam instantly — vaporizing it. The path left by the vaporized cells is much narrower than a cut from the smallest scalpel. That means less damage and faster healing for the patient. And the heat seals off blood vessels so there's less bleeding.

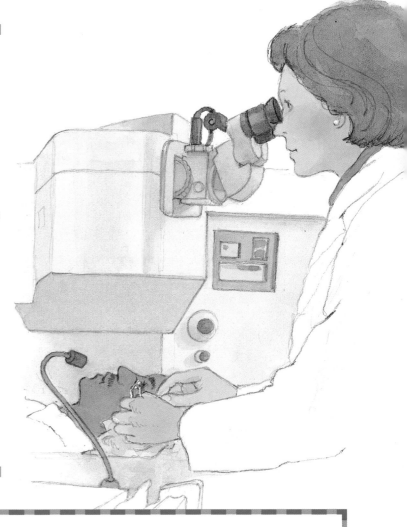

Vaporizing Cavities

Dentists may one day use lasers, too. Physicist Judith Dawes and her fellow researchers at Macquarie University in Sydney, Australia, have found a way to use painless lasers instead of drills to clean out cavities.

In the past, dentists worried that the energy from a laser would heat up healthy parts of the tooth and damage them. But Judith's team can now focus the laser's energy on just the decayed part of the tooth. First, they apply a dye that sticks to the decay only. Then they aim a laser of the right wavelength at that bad spot. While the rest of the tooth is unharmed, the dye and the decay under it absorb the energy until, zap! — your cavity is cleaned out and ready to be filled.

MAGIC MACHINES

"So, tell me again why we're at the mall info booth? Are there lasers here, too?" Kirsten asks, looking around the booth.

"Nope. At least, I don't think so. I wanted to see this touchscreen. I found out yesterday how it works. The engineer I talked to suggested I do an experiment to test one out," Gina explains.

"What about that one? Can we test it, too?" asks Kirsten, pointing to another machine.

"No, that's not a touchscreen. It has buttons and everything. This one doesn't have buttons, see? You just touch the screen. I'll try to remember what he said while we do the experiment, okay?"

2. The first kind the engineer told me about is called surface acoustic wave or SAW. In SAW touchscreens, sound waves travel across the glass all the time, but they're way too high-pitched for us to hear.

3. When I touch that kind of screen, my finger changes the sound waves.

Kind of like when you throw a stone in the water and the waves around it change to rings?

Right!

4. Then a thing in the machine's computer called the controller —

What's that?

It's like a translator. It senses where the sound wave changed and tells the computer exactly where you touched.

5. The engineer said touching a SAW screen gently with anything, even just a cloth, should trigger it.

Nothing happened.

Well, I guess we know this isn't a SAW screen.

6. What do we try now?

The second kind the engineer told me about is called a resistive screen. It has a special membrane just over top of the glass, but not touching it.

What's a membrane?

Like a thin sheet of plastic, I think.

7 The engineer said when you press firmly, you push the membrane and the glass together. The controller tells the computer where the two parts touched. Here. Try pressing with this pencil eraser.

Nothing. Guess this one isn't, uh, resistive either.

8 The last kind of screen is called capacitive. It has an electric current flowing to it all the time, trying to get to the ground.

Like how lightning always heads for the ground?

Yeah, except a touchscreen has only a tiny bit of electricity.

9 The engineer said when I touch a capacitive screen, the electricity finds its way through my finger, then my arm, my body and my legs into the ground.

Weird!

The controller can tell where I'm touching the screen by where the electric current escapes from the screen to the ground.

10 But why didn't the electricity flow through the cloth or pencil?

The engineer said, um ... Oh, yeah! Electricity only travels through certain materials, like our bodies and metal and water and stuff — unless there's a whole bunch of electricity, like in lightning.

11 Electricity can't get through rubber or plastic or a pencil or —

— cloth!

Right! Unless the cloth is wet. If this screen is capacitive, the electricity should be able to travel through this damp sponge and on through my body.

12

SELECT ONE
CLOTHING STORES
women's   outdoor
children's   footware

BACK TO MAIN MENU

Yes! It worked!

YOU'VE GOT THE TOUCH

Find a touchscreen in your community. They're used to update bank books, provide information in malls and cinemas, and even to make personalized greeting cards. Visit the touchscreen when no one is waiting to use it.

You'll need:

- ▶ a thick winter glove
- ▶ a folded facial tissue or cloth
- ▶ a pencil with an eraser
- ▶ a damp sponge
- ▶ a copy of the chart below

1. Touch the screen with your finger to see how easily it responds.

2. Touch the screen with the items on the list, one at a time. With your gloved finger, the facial tissue, the eraser and the sponge, barely touch the screen. Try again, this time pressing firmly. If the screen responds, mark a check in that space on the chart. If it doesn't respond, mark an X.

Check marks in all the "firm touch" spaces of your chart and none or maybe one in the "light touch" spaces, mean your touchscreen is probably resistive. If the check marks are under "damp sponge" only, the screen is capacitive. If you have check marks in almost all the spaces, the screen uses surface acoustic waves.

Test carefully. Some touchscreens react the moment you touch; others react as you release. Also, many touchscreens change by themselves to attract customers' attention. Mark a check in your chart only if the screen changes to what you asked to see.

	glove	tissue	pencil eraser	damp sponge
light touch				
firm touch				

SEE THE LIGHT

"How was the touchscreen test?" asks Gina's mom, as the girls climb in the car.

"Great! We figured out what kind of ..." Gina's voice trails off as the dozens of tiny words and symbols on the car dashboard light up.

"Gina?" her mom says, glancing at her.

"Sorry, Mom. I've seen these things light up a gazillion times, but how do they work? Is there a tiny lightbulb behind each one?"

Gina's mom shrugs. "I've never thought about it. Why don't you see what the car manual says?"

LIGHTS

The instrument panel indicators in this vehicle illuminate when the headlamps are switched on. Fiber-optic cables carry light from a single source inside the dashboard to many of the labels and symbols on the instrument panel surface.

34

WHAT ARE OPTICAL FIBERS?

Optical fibers are bendable strands of clear glass or plastic as thin as a hair. The glass core in an optical fiber is coated with another layer of glass called the cladding.

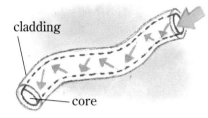

cladding

core

When you shine light inside a fiber, the surface where the cladding meets the core acts like a mirror, reflecting all the light back and forth along the fiber to the other end. This is called total internal reflection. Single optical fibers or bundles of several fibers can carry light around corners, underground — almost anywhere.

 CURVING LIGHT

Have you ever opened your eyes under calm water? If you look up in front of you, you don't see the sky. You see you! The bottom surface of the water reflects light down, just as the top reflects it up. Try this activity to see how a stream of water reflects light the way an optical fiber does.

You'll need:

▶ a large nail or metal skewer
▶ a large, clear plastic soda pop or juice bottle, label removed
▶ a flashlight
▶ water

1. Ask an adult to punch a hole with the nail in one side of the bottle, 5 cm (2 in.) up from the bottom.

2. With your finger over the hole, fill the bottle to about 10 cm (4 in.) above the hole. Stand the bottle on the edge of a sink, hole side in.

3. Turn off the lights and shine the flashlight through the side of the bottle opposite the hole.

4. Uncover the hole. Place your finger below the edge of the sink in the stream of water. Watch your fingertip as the water flows out.

That circle of light on your finger traveled down the stream of water, bouncing back and forth off the inside surface of the stream, just as light bounces inside a glass optical fiber. Some light spills out the sides of your stream of water, but good optical fibers carry all the light to the other end.

BUNDLES OF LIGHT

Since each tiny optical fiber can carry one small beam of light, bundles of them together can carry whole images, or pictures, too. Think of them as telescopes that can bend in any direction. Technicians use them to look inside nuclear reactors, jet engines, boilers and other places where it's not safe for a person to go.

The image of what's inside is shown on a monitor or directly on to a special visor that is connected to the fiber-optic tool. The fiber bundles are also good for looking into small or hard-to-reach places, such as pipes and machinery.

Leaf Light

Janet Bornman knows how well optical fibers carry light. Janet is a plant physiologist at Lund University in Lund, Sweden. That means she studies how plants grow and breathe. In her studies of how light affects plants, she needs to find out how much light her test plants absorb. Optical fibers are perfect for the job.

In Janet's lab, a special machine inserts one end of a very thin optical fiber just slightly into the underside of a leaf. The light that gets absorbed by the leaf travels

through the fiber to the other end, which Janet has hooked up to a light detector and a computer to help her measure how much light was absorbed. Voilà! A leaf light meter!

GET THE PICTURE?

Want to see how optical fibers carry a picture? Ask an adult if you can use a clear glass bowl, measuring cup or baking dish. Carefully tilt your dish so that you are looking into one edge. Hold a brightly colored object, such as a red plastic spoon, up to the opposite edge and move it slowly up and down.

Even though your glass dish is not an optical fiber bundle specially made for the job, it still carries a shadowy image of the object that you should be able to see on your edge of the dish. The image has bounced back and forth inside the glass shell — down, across the bottom of the dish and up to the other edge. If the glass in your dish is clear enough, you should even be able to see a hint of your object's color.

NATURAL FIBERS

Not all optical fibers are made by people: the polar bear is covered in natural optical fibers. Polar bear hairs aren't really white; they're clear. They only look white because of the light flowing through them. Sunlight travels along each hair to the polar bear's black skin, which absorbs the light and the warmth that comes with it. This neat trick of nature helps polar bears survive the Arctic's frigid weather.

IT'S WHAT'S INSIDE THAT COUNTS

"Roscoe's throwing up all over the house!" Sophie announces as Gina and her mom walk in the door.

"The vet suggested we bring him in," says Gina's dad, carrying the dog to the door. "He thinks Roscoe ate something he shouldn't have. Again."

Gina's dad sees the concern on her face. "Don't worry, honey," he adds gently, "Dr. McWatt says he can look into Roscoe's stomach to find out what the problem is."

"Poor guy. I hope you'll be okay," Gina murmurs, stroking Roscoe's head.

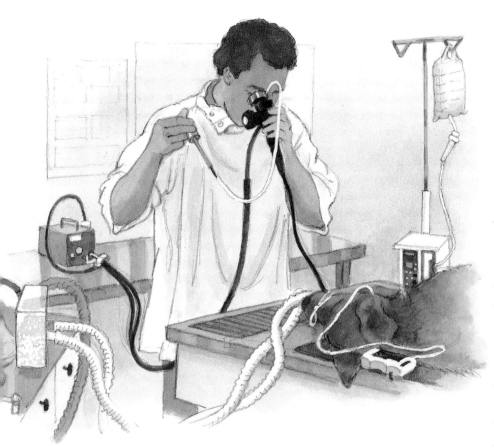

"This endoscope has optical fibers inside," Dr. McWatt explains, holding up what looks like a long, thin, black hose. "Light shines down some fibers to the end of the scope and other fibers carry the image back to the eyepiece. Once I slide the endoscope down into your dog's stomach, I'll be able to see the problem."

"But won't that hurt him?"

"Roscoe is asleep from the anesthetic. He won't feel anything."

"Are those endoscopes, too?" Gina wonders, pointing to the tubes hanging on the wall.

"Yes. The shorter, thinner ones are for small animals, such as kittens or guinea pigs. There are bigger ones for horses," explains Dr. McWatt, looking through the eyepiece. Moments later he says, "Yes, he's swallowed something."

"How will you get it out?" Gina worries.

"I'll feed this grabber down inside a tube in the endoscope. When I press a button, four wires slide out and separate. Then I release the button and the wires come together, grabbing the object. The optical fibers let me see what I'm doing. Once I have hold of it, I carefully pull out the endoscope and the object."

"Can the endoscope do other things, too?" asks Gina.

"Well, we can put another tool inside the scope to cut out small growths or to take tissue samples to test for diseases. Years ago, we would've had to operate on an animal to examine it or treat it for these things. An endoscope means the animal is back on its feet sooner." Dr. McWatt pauses. "I can see the object now."

"What did he swallow this time?" inquires Gina's dad.

"It looks like ... yes, it's a laser pointer. It'll be out in a few minutes."

"Oops," Gina says, looking guiltily at her dad. "Sorry."

THE INNER YOU

Doctors use endoscopes to help people, too. The optical fibers in these instruments let them see inside a patient's nasal passage, blood vessels, lungs and other hollow parts of the body. Surgeons can feed a laser tool through the endoscope's instrument channel to perform some surgeries without having to cut through the skin to get to the problem.

LONG-DISTANCE LIGHTS

Ms. Koffler shakes her head and smiles at Gina. "That's one way to learn about optical fibers. I'm glad your dog's okay." The teacher continues, "You know, there's another use of fiber optics that you haven't looked into yet, one we use many times every day."

Gina frowns. "What do we use many times every day? The stove, the car, the telephone — "

"Right!" says Ms. Koffler.

"Telephones? Oh, phone lines!" Gina's face lights up. "I think I'll go visit Mr. Ford in the library after school."

Telecommunication with fiber optics

In the past, people's voices were transmitted from telephone to telephone on electrical waves. Pulses of electricity surged through copper telephone cables.

Then the very small diode laser was invented. Researchers discovered that thin glass fibers could carry pulses of laser light — about 45 million flashes of light per second — and so transmit signals the same way copper wire carries electrical waves.

Not only could the optical fibers carry the same messages, but they could also carry them farther. In about 1985, telephone companies began replacing copper bundles with fiber-optic cables.

Improved fibers now carry many more signals than copper wires could. A pair of threadlike glass fibers can carry as many as one million telephone calls at once — it would take thousands and thousands of copper wires to transmit that many calls.

Fibers are now used to transmit more than voices. Through the Internet, these telephone cables carry sound, pictures and video clips from computer to computer, sometimes halfway around the world, in a matter of minutes. Who knows what else phone lines may transmit in the future?

96

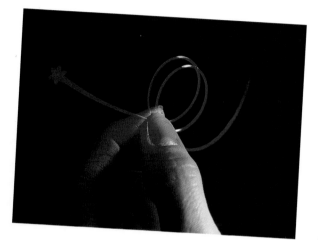

See the red light traveling along this coiled optical fiber? Normally, communication fibers transmit infrared laser light, which your eyes can't see.

97

Putting Fibers to the Test

Meet Terri Dixon, applications engineer. She works for a company in North Carolina, USA, that makes fiber-optic cables for office buildings and universities. The company wants to be sure that its cables keep transmitting communication signals, even if the cables are damaged. So part of Terri's job is beating up fiber-optic cables to see how much they can take and still work.

Terri uses special machines to twist, crush, bend, freeze and bake the cables. She sends signals into the test cables to see how much light gets through and how much leaks out because of the rough handling. If too much leaks out, the cables need to be improved.

EYES IN THE SKY

"You'd better wear your raincoat," Gina's mom says, as Gina heads for the door. "The radio announcer said it's going to rain."
"I don't see any clouds," grumbles Gina. "What makes him think it'll rain?"

"I think satellites must tell forecasters what the weather will be like. The announcer said something about 'satellite weather,'" replies her mom.

Sophie pipes up. "Cindy has a satellite in her backyard."

"That's a satellite *dish*," Gina tells her sister.

"Maybe when you get back you could see if your CD-ROM encyclopedia says anything about satellites," suggests Gina's mom.

WHAT IS A SATELLITE?

A satellite is any object that travels around, or orbits, a planet. Earth's Moon is a satellite, but usually when people talk about satellites, they mean manufactured objects that orbit Earth.

Satellites have solar panels that convert the light of the Sun into electricity. With that power, they perform many different jobs.

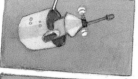

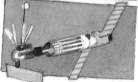

- Weather satellites transmit images of cloud patterns and measure temperature and moisture high in the atmosphere. This information helps weather specialists predict the weather.

- Search and rescue satellites listen for the frequency given off by all emergency beacons on ships and planes. If a ship is in trouble and its beacon transmits a signal, a satellite "hears" it and quickly notifies operators on the shore.

- Pictures from remote-sensing satellites help mapmakers produce accurate maps, or show tornado damage, holes in the ozone layer, dangerous levels of pollution and areas threatened by forest fires.

Some remote-sensing satellites face out, taking pictures and gathering information about outer space. Since they are outside Earth's atmosphere, they can "see" things telescopes on the ground can't see.

SATELLITES IN COMMUNICATION

Before satellites were invented, people used radio waves to communicate over oceans and mountains where there were no telephone cables. Operators would try to bounce a radio signal off the layers of gases in Earth's atmosphere to make the message travel farther, but this didn't always work.

It was a little like bowling in a lane that has a sharp turn partway down. Sometimes the ball bounces off the corner and heads for the pins, but often it just goes up over the side, out of the lane.

The very first satellites in the 1960s made continent-to-continent communication much more reliable. Transmitters sent radio waves up to a satellite that received the signal, amplified it (made it stronger) and relayed the signal down to another part of the Earth. The whole trip took about one quarter of a second.

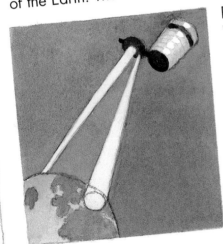

Before long, many countries had communications satellites in orbit. By 1976, communications satellites were being used to transmit live events all over the world.

Scientists think people may one day use satellites to collect solar energy, convert it to pollution-free electricity and send it back down to Earth.

SATELLITE SEARCH

Try this on a cloudless night when you are camping or far from a city or other source of lights. The satellites will be brighter and easier to see.

1. About an hour after dark, find a spot outdoors that gives a clear view of the sky.

2. Choose one area of the sky above you. Scan it slowly for at least ten minutes. Almost all of the points of light you see will be stars. Fast-moving or flashing points of light are probably airplanes.

3. If you detect a point of light moving silently and steadily across the sky, you've spotted a satellite.

What you are actually seeing is the Sun's light reflecting off the metal satellite, just as sunlight reflects off the Moon. With hundreds of satellites orbiting Earth, a little patience should be all you need to find one of these eyes-in-the-sky.

Where on Earth Am I?

The Global Positioning System (GPS) is a team of 24 satellites that helps sailors, pilots and some car drivers figure out exactly where they are. Elizabeth Cannon, an engineering professor at the University of Calgary in Canada, is a GPS specialist who writes computer programs that make these satellites useful.

GPS satellites send out signals all the time. A special antenna on a boat, plane or car receives signals from the GPS satellites in orbit above it. The boat's computer uses a program like the ones Elizabeth writes to figure out which satellites the signals are coming from, where those satellites are, and therefore where the boat must be.

MAKING WAVES

"Let's rent a comedy, okay, Dad?" Gina asks as they leave for the video store.

"Dad?" Sophie begins, watching the garage door go up.

Gina groans, "Come on, Sophie. No cartoons. You picked last time."

Sophie ignores her. "Dad, how did the garage door open by itself?"

"Hm. It opens when I press the button in the house," says their dad. "Any ideas, Gina?"

Gina thinks a moment. "Can't be infrared. The infrared from the TV remote bounced off paper instead of going through it, so I don't think it could go through a wall."

"I think I still have the manual," offers Gina's dad. "Let's see what it says."

No more fumbling for your keys in the rain!

Our remote garage door system lets you open your garage door from your car or home. Press the button on your remote and the unit sends a radio signal to the motor in your garage to open or close the door. Your system responds only to the specific radio signal of your remote.

Radio waves are invisible and can pass through brick walls and most other objects. They will not harm people or cause damage to your walls or car.

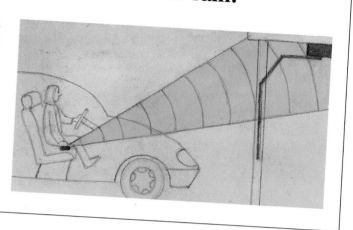

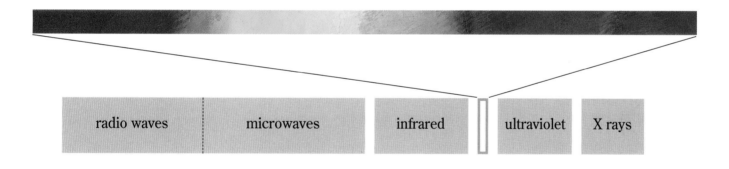

radio waves | microwaves | infrared | | ultraviolet | X rays

WHAT ARE RADIO WAVES?

Like infrared, radio waves are a type of electromagnetic radiation, or energy. But radio waves are much longer than infrared waves. Compare them on the chart.

When blue light waves (at the right end of the color band) travel through the air, about 10 million of them fit in a meter. Only about 1000 infrared waves fit in a meter because they are much longer. Radio waves are even longer. The shortest ones, called microwaves, are less than a centimeter long (more than 100 of them fit in a meter); the longest radio waves measure 10 million meters each.

Radio waves can carry a signal over short distances for things such as cordless telephones, remote control toys and baby monitors. With a stronger power source, radio waves can carry a signal farther to transmit radio station broadcasts, television shows and communications for police, firefighters, tow trucks and taxis.

✦ GETTING IN THE WAY

Radio waves can travel through walls and other objects, but those objects absorb part of the radio signal on its way through. The signal is like a beam of light: all of it passes through clear glass, but when it shines on cloth or colored plastic, only part of the beam gets through.

That's why, when you're in an underground parking garage, you may not be able to tune in any radio stations. The signal left after passing through the thick walls and the ground is too weak to hear clearly.

Do this test to find out what materials block radio waves.

You'll need:

▶ a radio remote control device (garage door opener, car door opener or remote control toy car) and permission to use it
▶ a cardboard box, a plastic tub or pail, a glass baking dish and a metal cookie tin or pot, each with a lid of the same material

1. Hold the garage door remote inside the box.

2. With your hand still on the remote, place the box lid over the opening as much as you can. (This is so the radio waves can't bounce out of the box.)

3. Aim the remote (in the box) at the garage and press a button. Does the garage door open? If it does, the box doesn't block radio waves.

4. Repeat with each of the other containers. Can radio waves travel through plastic? Glass? Metal?

Try this with walkie-talkies or a baby monitor. Place the receiver in the container. Can you hear a friend as she talks into the other part?

SECURITY GUARDS

Many stores and libraries use radio wave systems to stop thieves. Each store item has a tag or metal strip that picks up a certain radio signal. The exit gate has a receiver, too, as well as a radio transmitter that sends a continuous signal.

If someone leaves with an item, she hasn't paid for, she takes the item through the exit gate, where its tag picks up the transmitter's signal. The tag sends back a signal of its own, which sets off an alarm.

When you pay for your purchase, a clerk deactivates or removes the tag. Some video stores and libraries often just pass your selection to you around the exit gate, leaving the tag activated.

Directing Traffic

With police, taxis, tow trucks and many others using radio waves for communication, how do the right waves get to the right people? Ask Joanne McCourt, a radio frequency inspector with Canada's Department of Communications in Toronto.

Each company uses a certain frequency. That's the speed of radio waves used to carry a signal.

If a company wants to begin using radio waves to transmit information, Joanne's the person to contact. She analyzes the frequencies currently used in the area, then assigns the company a frequency that's compatible with everyone else's. That way, the signals don't interfere with one another.

COOKING WITH RADIO WAVES

"Mr. Ford showed me a library book," Gina tells her mom, "that says microwaves are just really short radio waves. It makes me wonder how our microwave oven works."

"And why it doesn't play music, right?" her mom jokes. Then she continues, "Maybe you should see if that Ask an Expert Web site has the answer."

"Good idea! Can I use your computer?"

HERE'S WHAT OUR EXPERT SAID

Every microwave oven contains a machine called a magnetron. It uses electricity to produce electromagnetic energy in very short radio waves, called microwaves. The waves of energy pass through a sort of tunnel called a waveguide to a fan that bounces them into all parts of the oven. The waves bounce off the metal walls of the oven and pass through most containers into the food being cooked.

The microwaves are just the right frequency to be absorbed by tiny bits (molecules) of water that are in all food. The energy makes the molecules of water twist around, or vibrate, very quickly and that warms up the food around them. The more microwaves that enter the food, the more the food warms up.

magnetron

TRY THIS!   **BACK TO TOPICS**

*Forgotten where microwaves are on the electromagnetic spectrum? Turn to page 47.

TRY THIS!
SEE MICROWAVES AT WORK
You'll need:
- a microwave oven and permission to use it
- a glass that can safely go in a microwave oven
- a large bowl that can go in a microwave oven
- unpopped popcorn • water • oven mitts

1. Sit the glass in the bowl. Pour a large spoonful of popcorn into the glass.
2. Add water to the bowl to about one third of the way up the glass.
3. Put the bowl in the microwave. Turn it on high power for 90 seconds.
4. Ask an adult with oven mitts to carefully remove the bowl. Did the popcorn pop? Can you feel heat rising from the water? (Do not touch the water.)
5. Pour out the water and replace the popcorn in the glass with a fresh spoonful the same size. Repeat the experiment.

WHAT HAPPENED?   **BACK TO TOPICS**

WHAT HAPPENED?

The first time you turned the oven on, the microwaves were absorbed by the many water molecules in the bowl, vibrating each a little. This made the water warm up. When you remove the water, all the microwaves go into the only water that's left: the molecules inside each popcorn kernel. That water heats up, expands as it turns to steam, and POP! — you've got popcorn.

WIRELESS WONDERS

"... So, many cellular telephones and pagers use both radio waves and satellites," Gina explains, nearing the end of her presentation. "Take a look at my last poster to see a picture of how they work."

WIRELESS COMMUNICATION

When I use our cell phone to call my dad's pager, the phone changes my message into radio waves. This radio signal travels from the phone's antenna to a nearby tower called a transmitter. The transmitter passes the signal to the closest cellular telephone switching office (a place that connects different types of phone calls).

The cellular switching office relays the radio wave message up to a satellite. The satellite sends the message down to all the transmitters in the pager's area, which broadcast the radio wave message out to all pagers. Because I dialed my dad's pager number, my dad's pager is the one that gets my message.

Not all pager messages or cellular calls go through a satellite. Some companies just use cables and radio waves to send out their signals.

Gina stops and looks around. No one looks confused! She takes a deep breath and reads her last paragraph: "The field of advanced technology just keeps growing. Who knows what strange and wonderful examples of technology may be part of our everyday lives in the future."

"That was excellent!" says Ms. Koffler, just as the bell rings.

"Yeah!" Kirsten agrees, then asks, "Hey, do you know anything about DVD movies? My brother says you can play them on your computer or on your TV."

"Sounds like a good topic for the science fair," suggests Ms. Koffler.

"What do you think, Gina? Want to be partners?" asks Kirsten.

"Sure!" Gina smiles. Suddenly, she realizes, advanced technology doesn't seem like such a mystery.

WHAT'S YOUR NUMBER?

You sit, clenching a bingo chip in your hand. Will the next number called match the one left on your bingo card?

Believe it or not, cell phones and pagers are a little like bingo players. As long as they are turned on, these gizmos wait and listen to see if their number is being called. They "hear" lots of other numbers go by, but only when their number is called do they spring into action, ringing or vibrating to let you know that someone wants to talk to you.

SCIENCE FAIR PROJECTS

Looking for some science fair project ideas about everyday technology? Here are more activities you can do that involve or further explain some of the technologies you've read about in this book.

Infrared

Black objects absorb infrared (see page 9). To prove it, line two matching cardboard boxes, one with black construction paper, the other with shiny aluminum foil. Rub your hands together to warm them. Place one hand in each box, palm up about 2.5 cm (1 in.) from the top. After ten seconds or so, switch them. Then switch them back. Feel the difference? Which box absorbs your body's infrared, leaving your palm feeling cooler? Which one reflects it?

Lasers

Specific wavelengths of laser light are absorbed by some materials and not by others (see page 29). Shine a laser pointer through a clear pan full of red jelly dessert and another full of blue. (NEVER SHINE A LASER INTO ANYONE'S EYES.) Which color transmits, or passes along, the pointer's red light and which absorbs it?

Fiber Optics

If a communication signal enters a fiber-optic cable at the correct angle, all of that signal travels to the cable's other end (see page 35). If the signal enters at the wrong angle, a part of it leaks out. Shine a small flashlight or a laser pointer at a window or other flat piece of glass. Aim it straight at the glass and the light shines right through. Aim it at an angle and some light goes through while some bounces off. Record what the light does at different angles. Can you find the best angle for total internal reflection?

Microwaves

Water absorbs microwaves (see page 51). After the same time in a microwave oven, which do you think will be warmer — food with lots of water in it or food with little water? Microwave, together, a wet sample and a dry sample of a few different foods — such as a dry cracker and one you have dipped in water — and record how each is affected. Remember to use the same temperature and the same quantity of each food.

Touchscreens

Find a capacitive touchscreen (see page 32). This type is fairly common. What objects will conduct, or pass along, the electric current and trigger the screen? (These objects are called conductors.) A banana? Cardboard? A metal spoon? A plastic spoon? Keep track of which ones are conductors.

Radio Waves

Radio signals can be heard much farther away if they bounce off the atmosphere (see page 44). Do radio signals bounce more during the day or at night? Does the weather affect them? Start at one end of a radio's AM tuning dial and move slowly to the other. Record the time and weather and the dial number of each station you find and whether it is faint or clear. Do this on two or three different days at noon and, with permission, late at night.

⭐ Satellites

With an SLR camera (one that lets you hold the shutter open), a tripod and some luck, you can take pictures of satellites. Load the camera with 400 ASA film. An hour after sunset on a cloudless night, find a place outdoors away from lights. Mount the camera on the tripod so the camera points up but away from the Moon. Open the iris to f-stop 1.8 and focus on the stars. Set the shutter speed to "B," then watch the sky (not through the camera).

When you see a satellite passing above the camera, gently press and hold the shutter for 30 seconds. (Don't jiggle the camera.) You may have to try quite a few times. Tell the clerk at the photo shop what you're doing so she can make sure the very dark shots are developed. A satellite will show up as a pale, straight line against the background of stars.

Note to Parents, Teachers and Group Leaders

Technology is advancing faster than at any other time in history. The world is suddenly filled with satellites, fax machines, cellular phones and many other items now essential to businesses as well as homes. With so much change, specialists estimate that by the time today's kindergarten students enter the workforce, 90 percent of the available jobs will be ones that don't even exist today.

Traditionally, girls have been less likely than boys to enter fields of advanced technology. In 1999, less than 20 percent of all undergraduate engineering students in the United States were female. For various reasons, girls seem to get "turned off" most types of science at an early age. If science is not made more relevant to them, they may be left behind their male peers as technology rushes forward.

This book aims to inspire girls and make them comfortable with the technology that surrounds them. When they realize that these gadgets work using concepts they can understand, young girls may see technology as something fascinating to learn more about, something that affects them every day.

The profiles in the book, which introduce women who work with these technologies, are included to help girls realize that they, too, can consider careers in technology.

Most importantly, the book's goal is to help young readers, boys as well as girls, begin to ask their own questions about the technological "mysteries" around them, and to pique their curiosity about the scientific marvels normally taken so much for granted.

INDEX